Master Scholars
Tutoring & Test Prep

Master Scholars SAT* Math Student Workbook
For the NEW SAT – Out March 2016!

By: Jesse Patrick

*SAT is a registered trademark of the College Board, which was not involved in the production of, and does not endorse, this product.

Master Scholars SAT Student Workbook

Copyright © 2015 Master Scholars Tutoring and Test Prep. All rights reserved.

No part of this publication may be reproduced, stored, or transmitted in any form or by any means (electronic or mechanical, including photocopying, recording, or by any other information storage and retrieval system) without prior written permission of the copyright holder.

Although reasonable effort has been taken to ensure the accurate presentation of reliable and useful information in this book, the author assumes no responsibility for errors or omissions. Further, no liability is assumed for any damages resulting from the use of information contained herein.

All information contained herein is provided "AS IS", for informational purposes only. The challenging nature of the topic and reliance on outside sources for information prevents us from giving any warranty or guarantee either expressed or implied that the information appearing herein or accessible through links to outside sources will be accurate, complete, current, relevant, or timely in content. We further make no warranties either expressed or implied as to the quality or accuracy of any information contained herein and do not make any claims as to the use of this information for any particular purposes(s).

SAT and SAT Reasoning Test are registered trademarks of the College Board. PSAT/NMSQT is a registered trademark of the College Board and National Merit Scholarship Corp. Neither the College Board nor National Merit Scholarship Corp. has endorsed nor is in any way affiliated with this publication of Master Scholars Test Prep, LLC.

The Official SAT Study Guide is © 2015 by the College Board and Educational Testing Service, and is not a publication of Master Scholars Test Prep, LLC.

Written by Jesse Patrick

More information and Video Series available at www.masterscholars.com

Table of Contents:

HOW TO USE THIS BOOK   pg. 4

SAT INTRO   pg. 5-8

- Basic Strategies   pg. 9-14
    - Vocabulary   pg. 9
    - Plugging In   pg. 10-11
    - Working Backwards   pg. 11
    - Converting Equations   pg. 12
    - Bite-Sized Pieces   pg. 13
    - Process of Elimination   pg. 13

- Arithmetic/Statistics   pg. 15-22
    - Rates/Ratios/Conversions   pg. 15-16
    - Percentages   pg. 17
    - Two-Way Frequency Charts   pg. 18
    - Mean, Median, Mode, and Range   pg. 19-21
    - Read Data and Make Conclusions   pg. 22

- Algebra 1   pg. 23-32
    - Solving Equations/Inequalities   pg. 23-24
    - Slope   pg. 25
    - Equations of Lines   pg. 26-28
    - Systems of Equations/Inequalities   pg. 29-31
    - Finding a Graph to Match a Situation   pg. 32

- Geometry   pg. 33-44
    - Geometry Basics/Volume   pg. 33-36
    - Right Triangles   pg. 37-38
    - Triangles   pg. 39-41
    - Circles   pg. 42-44

- Algebra 2/Advanced Topics   pg. 45-57
    - Functions and Applications   pg. 45-46
    - Quadratics Functions   pg. 47-49
    - Polynomials   pg. 50-51
    - Exponential Functions   pg. 52-53
    - Radical/Rational Functions   pg. 54-55
    - Complex Numbers   pg. 56
    - Line/Curve of Best Fit   pg. 57

How To Use This Book:

Thank you for your interest in SAT prep from Masters Scholars. This complete SAT tutorial is unique but equally effective. By basing our content off of the exact questions from the College Board, this book gives you the best indicator of what you will see on test day. Before getting started lets quickly review how this book works.

This book covers all the different math topics that show up on the SAT. The book was written to be used with the Master Scholars Video Series. **If you purchased this book and do not currently have the video series, you must contact Jesse Patrick at masterscholarstestprep@gmail.com. State that you have purchased the book you will be given the information to obtain the video series.** Most sections are broken down into categories that detail specific test strategies. At the end of each topic, you will see a chart that looks like this:

Topics	
Test #1	
Sec. 3	
Sec. 4	
Test #2	
Sec. 3	
Sec. 4	
Test #3	
Sec. 3	
Sec. 4	
Test #4	
Sec. 3	
Sec. 4	

Each chart references the 4 Practice Tests issued by The CollegeBoard/Khan Academy. After you have learned a topic or strategy, use the chart to try official SAT questions! This is an easy and effective guide to easily master the SAT!

Easy enough right? Well, lets get started then!

SAT INTRODUCTION

DON'T HAVE THE VIDEO SERIES YET? E-MAIL
Masterscholarstestprep@gmail.com now!

SAT stands for: _____ _____ _____

College Board began way back in 1901. In 1926, the College Board administered their first SAT, which at the time stood for the Scholastic Aptitude Test. But in 1990, because of uncertainty about the SAT's ability to function as an intelligence test, the name was changed to Scholastic Assessment Test. In 1993 the name was changed to SAT I: Reasoning Test (with the letters not standing for anything) to distinguish it from the SAT II: Subject Tests. In 2004, the roman numerals on both tests were dropped, and the SAT I was renamed the SAT Reasoning Test. In response to threats by the University of California to drop the SAT as an admission requirement, the College Entrance Examination Board announced the restructuring of the SAT, to take effect in March 2005. The new SAT added a writing component in addition to its reading and math sections. The old perfect score of a 1600 was changed to a 2400. More recently, David Coleman became the president of the CollegeBoard. Coleman is one of the founding fathers of Common Core, so his first order of business was to make the SAT in his likeness; it didn't hurt that the ACT was also overtaking the SAT in terms of popularity. Therefore, in March 2016, and October of 2015 for the PSAT, the SAT underwent ANOTHER change, and is now more focused on the Common Core Standards. So in short, now we can make up our own name for the SAT; isn't history great!

The Format:

Timing: 3 hours and 50 minutes (including the optional 50 minute essay)
READING TEST: 65 minutes, 52 questions
WRITING AND LANGUAGE ARTS TEST: 35 minutes, 44 questions
MATH TEST:
    Non-calculator section: 25 minutes, 20 questions
    Calculator section: 55 minutes, 38 questions
ESSAY: 50 minutes

Sections: 1 evidenced-based reading
1 evidence-based writing
2 math (one with calculator and one without)
1 essay (optional)

Question Types: 141 multiple choice
13 grid-in (math only)

Penalty: There is no more penalty for guessing. Answer EVERYTHING!

Scoring: Total score ranges from 400-1600 (200-800 per section)
Essay score reported separately
Subscores and cross-test scores issued to show more specific skills/deficiencies

Scoring:

Test Scores: 10-40 for Reading, Writing, and Math
Area Scores: 200-800 for Evidence-Based Reading and Writing
Composite Scores: 400-1600 for Math (Area Score) + Reading and Writing (Area Score)
Essay Scores: 1-4

  The final SAT score that will matter will be the composite score. The test scores will be used to help you determine what areas you need to work on to improve your scores. There will also be cross-section scores, which will take questions that you answers from various sections, and use those to determine general weaknesses, such as analytical reasoning based on chart questions from reading and math. Area specific sub-scores will also be provided, which will list the types of questions missed by topic within on particular test.

What's on it:

Math: Arithmetic
    Ratios, percentage problems, basic statistics, etc…
  Algebra 1 and 2
    Solving equations and systems of equations, equations of lines, including questions on the following types of functions: quadratics, exponentials, radicals, rationals, and polynomials.
  Geometry
    Volume, triangles, trig ratios (yes, this is a Geometry topic), circle properties, etc…

English: Passage-Based Reading (Long and Short single and dual passages) and Grammar in context

Writing: 50-minute essay

Scoring Scale:

200-800

> Set up an account on www.Collegeboard.org and search some colleges!

An average score is typically a 500 per section, or 1000 overall.

What do I need to score on the test?

It's important for you to start thinking about what your scoring goal should be. If you don't have an SAT score yet, take your PSAT score and add a 0 to it (for example, a 54 on math would equal a 540 on the SAT). If you haven't take the PSAT, take a practice test through CollegeBoard or Khan Academy. Do a college search at www.Collegeboard.org and start looking at colleges and what kind of scores they are looking for. Just remember that it is great motivation to have a target score in mind.

Once you have come up with a target score, go ahead and write it down HERE:

MATH: ENGLISH:

How many questions do I need to answer correctly to achieve my goal?

Using the scoring chart at the end of test one in the Official SAT Study Guide, look at the number of questions right needed for each section. Once you find your score for each subsection, list those numbers below.

MATH: ENGLISH:

How does the average scorer do on the test?
  Easy Questions:

  ~ 90% correct

  Medium Questions:

  ~ 50% correct

  Hard Questions:

  ~ 0% correct (this is not a typo!)

If every student received a perfect score on the SAT, then it wouldn't be a very good "norming" test, would it? Therefore, the SAT designs questions that they expect most students to get wrong; they do this a number of ways, which include difficult vocabulary, tricky sentence errors, rarely used math formulas, etc. Learning these tricks is the key to raising your score, so even though the hard questions will typically give you the most headaches, most of your effort should be on mastering those hardest questions.

PSAT/NMSQT:

The PSAT/NMSQT is not just a warm-up to the SAT…I mean it is, but there is so much more to it than that. That NMSQT portion at the end of the test name stands for National Merit Scholarship Qualifying Test. You have the option of taking the test during your freshmen, sophomore, and junior year of High School. However, your junior year PSAT is the only test that will qualify you for National Merit. In order to become a National Merit Finalist, your PSAT scores must be in the top 1% in the state. It is free to take the PSAT as a sophomore, which is important since it will show you where you match up with the rest of the students in the country. You also will receive a test booklet with your score results which will be an invaluable resource as you prepare for the PSAT your junior year, although this time it will cost you about $20 to take it.

When to take the SAT:

Most students take the SAT during the spring of their junior year, but because of College Boards "Score Choice Option", it can be beneficial to take it early. Score Choice basically means that you have the option of sending your best scores to colleges. So by taking the test multiple times, you have more than one chance to get your desired score. While some schools may ask to see all your test scores, most of those schools still only consider your top score.

My normal suggested progression is based on another valuable program offered by College Board, and that is the SAT QAS (Question and Answer Service). Through the QAS, you have the option of ordering a copy of the test along with your score report three times a year. The only tests that have the QAS option are the October, January, and May administrations.

Therefore, my suggestion is to take the SAT in October of your Junior year. This test is like a warm up; see how you do and heck, you may even surprise yourself. After some additional prep on your trouble points and a review of your October SAT take the test again in January. If you are still not happy or you feel that you can get even higher, keep reviewing your prep work and your January SAT and take the test in May. What is nice about this progression is that you still have the option of taking the test again in October of your Senior year, although I am sure most of you will have had enough at that point (which is totally understandable I may add).

Just understand that this is just a suggestion and every student is different. If you're not ready when you start your Junior year, then don't waste your time taking the test in October. Do you feel ready as a Sophomore and want to see how you do? Take the test early and get a head start on your classmates!

How to Register:

PSAT: See your school counselor

SAT: Go to www.collegeboard.org and click on SAT

ACT: Go to www.ACTStudent.org

Basic Strategies

DON'T HAVE THE VIDEO SERIES YET? E-MAIL
Masterscholarstestprep@gmail.com now!

Before we get started with real, tried and true math, let's make sure that you are aware of typical math vocabulary and some strategies that we will use throughout the course.

Term	Definition	Example
Integer	A non-fractional rational number	….-3, -2, -1, 0, 1, 2, 3, …
Distinct	Different	Five "distinct" integers: -2, 0, 3, 5, and 7
Even	Integers that are divisible by 2	…, -4, -2, *0*, 2, 4, …
Odd	Integers that are not divisible by 2	…-3, -1, 1, 3, …
Difference	Subtraction	The "difference" between 3 and 5 is 2.
Sum	Addition	The "sum" of 3 and 5 is 8.
Product	Multiplication	The "product" of 3 and 5 is 15.
Quotient	Division	The "quotient of 15 and 5 is 3.
Consecutive	One after another	Four "consecutive" positive even integers are 2, 4, 6, and 8. (0 is neither positive or negative).
Prime	Numbers that are divisible by only 1 and itself. 1 IS NOT PRIME! The only even prime number is 2 (since all other even numbers would be divisible by 2!).	The prime numbers less than 30 are: 2, 3, 5, 7, 11, 13, 17, 19, 23, and 29.
Inclusive	Including	The numbers from 3 to 5 "inclusive" are 3, 4, and 5.
Factor	The terms that multiply to give you a larger integer. **Commonly used on exponential equation questions***	48 ∧ 16 3 ∧ 4 4 ∧ ∧ 2 2 2 2 The prime factors of 48 are 2 and 3.
Digit	The parts of a number. Digits are ALWAYS denoted with capital letters on the SAT. 2a = "2 times a" while 2A = "twenty something".	ABC = 237 Hundreds Digit: 2 Tens Digit: 3 Units Digit: 7

Plugging In:

Plugging in turns algebra problems into arithmetic problems. The ultimate goal is to reduce the difficulty of the problem.

For example:

Suppose you are at a hardware store and buy 6 bolts at 5 cents each. You give the clerk $1. How much change do you receive?

70¢

Suppose you buy 12 bolts for 15 cents a piece. You give the clerk $2. How much change do you receive now?

20¢

NOW, let's say you buy p bolts for c cents a piece. You give the clerk d dollars. Now what is your change?

$d \cdot 100 - p \cdot c$

Times to Plug-In:
1. When there are **variables in the answer choices** and/or the phrase **"in terms of"** is used in the question
2. When the question asks you to find a **fraction** or a **percent**.
    a. For percent plug-in's, always plug in 100 or 10.
3. If the word "could" or "must" is used, be prepared to use more than one number.
    a. Must: Answer must **always** work
    b. Could: Answer **only needs to work once**.
4. Always be aware to pick numbers that work well in the problem. Avoid using "0" or "1" whenever possible on **Multiple Choice Plug-in's**. On Grid-ins, picking 0 or 1 is allowed! (yippee!!!)

If $\frac{x}{y} = 6$, what is the value of $\frac{12y}{7x}$?

(A) $\frac{1}{7}$
(B) $\frac{2}{7}$
(C) $\frac{24}{49}$
(D) $\frac{72}{7}$

At a recent employee sale, Jason bought a pair of shoes at 25% off the stores price. The amount he paid the cashier was y dollars, which included the 6% sales tax. In terms of y, which of the following represents the original price of the shoes?

(A) $.25y$
(B) $.69y$
(C) $(.25)(1.06)y$
(D) $\frac{y}{(.75)(1.06)}$

In the equation, $V = \pi r^2 h$, volume V of a right circular cylinder is equal to the radius, r, squared times the height, h, and pi. With all other components remaining the same, if a person finds that the radius of cylinder A is 5 times greater than the radius of cylinder B, then the volume of cylinder A would be what fraction of the volume of cylinder B?

(A) $\frac{1}{50}$
(B) $\frac{1}{25}$
(C) $\frac{2}{25}$
(D) $\frac{1}{5}$

A rectangle is to be altered by increasing its length by 20 percent and decreasing its width by 30 percent. What effect will this have on the area of the rectangle?

(A) The area will decrease by 16%.
(B) The area will decrease by 15%.
(C) The area will increase by 15%.
(D) The area will increase by 16%.

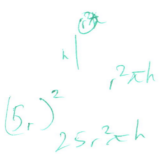

Working Backwards (PITA):

When to Work Backwards:
1) When the question is **asking for a variable**.
   a. If you think about it, one of your answers is the variable!
2) When the phrase "**which if the following**" is used in the question.
3) Any other time that your answers can be plugged back into the problem.
Since most answers are listed in order, start with B or C and plug it back in to the question to see if it works.
   If your choice is too large, eliminate the larger answers.
   If your choice is too small, eliminate smaller answers.
   Obviously if your answers choice works then you've found your answer.
       When you find the correct answer, STOP!

If $(a - b)^a = 0$ and $b^a = 1$, where a and b are positive integers, what is the value of a?

(A) 1
(B) 2
(C) 3
(D) 4

A container is $\frac{2}{5}$ full of water. If 4 gallons of the water were added to the container, it would be $\frac{1}{2}$ full. How many gallons of water does this container hold when it is completely full?

(A) 10
(B) 24
(C) 40
(D) 120

Converting Equations:

ENGLISH	MATH EQUIVALENT
% (Percent)	÷100
X% more (ex. 20% more)	Multiply by 1.## (multiply by 1.20)
of	Multiply
what	Variable
is, are, were, did, does, results	Equal sign
More	Addition
Less	Subtraction
Twice	Multiply by two
Per	Divide

The SAT will try to mess with your head by explaining equations rather than just giving them to you. Focus on the words, and then write the equations down and do the math! Here are a few easier ones to warm up on before trying the problems listed in the chart.

20 percent of what number is 50?

a) 25
b) 70
c) 100
d) 250

What percent of 50 is 225?

a) 45
b) 200
c) 250
d) 450

What number is 50% more than 45?

a) 22.5
b) 45
c) 62.5
d) 67.5

Bite-Sized-Pieces:

Don't be overwhelmed when you see a long word problem. College Board expects you to rush through the question and get confused. You need to attack long questions in little chunks. When there's something to figure out, STOP! Figure out what they are giving you before moving on. Learn to attack problems in this way. In addition, learn to read the question and underlining key words or phrases as you go; it will make it easier to find that information later when you need it.

For their graduation ceremony, the 50 students in Jennifer's senior class were each assigned a different whole number from 1 to 50. Jennifer and her classmates entered the auditorium in numerical order, and every 10 students filled a different row, maintaining that order. There were aisles on both ends of each row, and only one student sat between Jennifer and the aisle. Which of the following CANNOT be Jennifer's number?

(A) 12
(B) 24
(C) 39
(D) 42

A bookstore has 15000 books in stock, of which 60 percent are paperback and 40 percent are hardcover. All the books are either fiction or nonfiction. If 4500 of the books are nonfiction and 2500 of the nonfiction books are paperback, how many of the books are both fiction and hardcover?

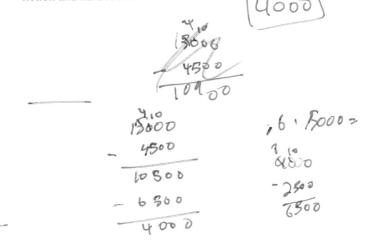

Process of Elimination:

Process of Elimination, or POE, is a commonly used strategy for all sections of the SAT. In terms of the math section, POE can be extremely useful when you are having trouble with a problem. Since there is no penalty for guessing, it is in your best interests to answer every question. In order to increase your chances of getting the question right, it is best to try to eliminate answers that you know are wrong. Here are just a couple of examples where you can use process of elimination to your advantage.

At Lyman High School, Calculus students were asked, "What is your favorite subject in school?". Five students were absent that day and two failed to respond. If the survey was conducted at the end of the school day, which factor makes it the least likely that a reliable conclusion would be made?

(A) The survey was done at the end of the day
(B) The number of people who didn't respond
(C) The students who were absent
(D) The sample population

If x is a negative odd integer and y is a positive even integer, which of the following could be equal to $x + y$?

I. 0
II. 1
III. 2

(A) I only
(B) II only
(C) III only
(D) I and III only

Basic Strategies Homework:

Plugging In	
Test #1	
Sec. 3	8
Sec. 4	20
Test #2	
Sec. 3	
Sec. 4	23
Test #3	
Sec. 3	
Sec. 4	27
Test #4	
Sec. 3	
Sec. 4	

Working Backwards	
Test #1	
Sec. 3	1
Sec. 4	10
Test #2	
Sec. 3	
Sec. 4	
Test #3	
Sec. 3	
Sec. 4	
Test #4	
Sec. 3	
Sec. 4	

Converting Equations	
Test #1	
Sec. 3	
Sec. 4	4
Test #2	
Sec. 3	
Sec. 4	6
Test #3	
Sec. 3	4
Sec. 4	22
Test #4	
Sec. 3	
Sec. 4	34

Bite-Sized Pieces	
Test #1	
Sec. 3	
Sec. 4	
Test #2	
Sec. 3	
Sec. 4	
Test #3	
Sec. 3	
Sec. 4	5
Test #4	
Sec. 3	
Sec. 4	3

Process of Elimination (POE)	
Test #1	
Sec. 3	
Sec. 4	
Test #2	
Sec. 3	
Sec. 4	13
Test #3	
Sec. 3	15
Sec. 4	
Test #4	
Sec. 3	
Sec. 4	26

Arithmetic/Statistics

Rates/Ratios/Conversions:

A ratio is <u>not</u> just a fraction, but a relationship between two or more things. Ratios can be compared through a **proportion**. When working with a proportion, remember the following property to solve.

$$\frac{a}{b} = \frac{c}{d} \longrightarrow ad = bc$$

While this may not always be the case, many proportion questions include the phrase "at this rate".

Also note, that the ratio $a\ to\ b = a:b = \frac{a}{b}$

On a certain map, 3 inches represent 20 miles. How many inches on the map represent 100 miles?

(A) 3
(B) 6
(C) 15
(D) 50

If $\frac{4}{x} = 20$, what is the value of $\frac{1}{x} - x$?

(A) 0
(B) .04
(C) 4
(D) 4.8

If $\frac{6}{x} = \frac{10}{x+2}$, what is the value of $\frac{x}{6}$?

(A) $\frac{1}{3}$
(B) $\frac{1}{2}$
(C) 2
(D) 3

A machine at a horseradish plant produces 7 bottles of horseradish in 20 seconds. At this rate, how many bottles of horseradish will the machine produce in 2 hours?

(A) 14
(B) 140
(C) 2520
(D) 8400

As seen in the last example, another use for ratios is conversions. Conversions can be done using **conversion factors**.

> 1 Liter = 2.1 Pints

An adult male contains 12 pints of blood. How many liters of blood are there in a typical adult male?

(A) 3.1
(B) 5.7
(C) 14.1
(D) 24.2

A go-kart travels 23 miles per hour. Convert this speed into feet per second.

(A) .06
(B) 24.5
(C) 33.7
(D) 2024

Finally, the SAT will seldom require the use of the following formula: D = RT (Distance = Rate x Time). Pay attention to problems that list the three variables; distance, rate, and time. Once you recognize the problem, fill in the missing variables and solve!

If it takes 10 minutes to travel from point A to point B at a constant speed of 30 miles per hour, how many minutes does it take to travel the same route from point A to point B at a constant speed of 20 miles per hour?

A passenger plane made a trip to Kansas City and back. On the trip there it flew 410 miles per hour and on the return trip it traveled 386 miles per hour. Which of the following is the closest to the time that it took the plane to travel to Kansas City if the return trip took 2.7 hours

(A) 2.52
(B) 2.67
(C) 3.13
(D) 3.35

Rates/Ratios/Conversions	
Test #1	
Sec. 3	
Sec. 4	6
Test #2	
Sec. 3	
Sec. 4	2, 15, 31, 32
Test #3	
Sec. 3	5
Sec. 4	9, 19
Test #4	
Sec. 3	6
Sec. 4	4, 31, 33

Percentages:

When working with percentages, remember your rules for converting equations. In addition to those rules, here are a couple of phrases that the SAT likes to use when dealing with percentages.

Phrase	Example	Decimal Equivalent
Percent more	35 percent more	1.35
Percent less	35 percent less	.65 (1 - .35)

Likewise, the SAT will tend to use phrases such as, "55% of the students earned A's, 25% earned B's, and the rest earned C's. How many students earned C's?" Of course, in this situation you have to calculate the percentage of C's (20%) and use that in your calculation. Here are some examples.

Two runners are racing each other. Runner A can run 30% faster than runner B. If runner A ran 9.6 miles in 1 hour, how far did runner B run?

(A) .14
(B) 6.7
(C) 7.4
(D) 12.48

Two runners are racing each other. Runner A runs 30% slower than runner B. If runner B ran 9.6 miles in 1 hour, how far did runner B run?

(A) .14
(B) 6.7
(C) 7.4
(D) 12.48

Finally, the SAT will, from time to time, require the use of the following formula for percent change:

$$percent\ change = \frac{difference}{original}$$

In America, the median income of a high school graduate is $26,505 and the median income of a college graduate is $49,303. A college graduate with a master's degree will earn a median income of $52,390. What is the percent increase in income from students earning a high school diploma to those earning a master's degree?

(A) 46%
(B) 49%
(C) 86%
(D) 98%

Working With Percentages	
Test #1	
Sec. 3	
Sec. 4	26
Test #2	
Sec. 3	
Sec. 4	5 (if stuck, do after eqn. of lines), 17
Test #3	
Sec. 3	
Sec. 4	
Test #4	
Sec. 3	
Sec. 4	22

Two-Way Frequency Charts:

If you have a data set with two categorical variable, you can list the frequencies of the paired values in a two-way frequency table. When you encounter these charts, you can most likely skip half the question, because every chart question on the SAT wastes your time by describing the chart. While it is important to be able to read a two-way frequency table, you also need to be comfortable with probability.

$$Probability = \frac{Number\ of\ desired\ outcomes}{Total\ possible\ outcomes}$$

Be sure to pay attention WHERE the desired outcomes are coming from, and from what total.

For the following examples, use the following two-way frequency chart:

SAT RESULTS FROM HIGH SCHOOL JUNIORS

	Score Went Down	Score Did Not Change	Score Went Up	Total
Took SAT Prep Class	5	2	13	
Did Not Take SAT Prep Class	8	15	3	
Total				

The table above shows the results from High School juniors on their SAT exam. If one of the students whose score went up was chosen at random, what is the probability that they took the SAT Prep class?

(A) .81
(B) .65
(C) .28
(D) .13

The table above shows the results from High School juniors on their SAT exam. If one of the students whose chosen at random, what is the probability that their score either went down or did not change?

(A) .12
(B) .35
(C) .65
(D) .88

Two Way Frequency Charts	
Test #1	
Sec. 3	
Sec. 4	13 , 21
Test #2	
Sec. 3	
Sec. 4	16
Test #3	
Sec. 3	
Sec. 4	2
Test #4	
Sec. 3	
Sec. 4	7, 9

Mean, Median, Mode, and Range:

Mean – Otherwise known as an average or an arithmetic mean (NOTE, the SAT <u>always</u> denotes these types of problems with the phrase, "average (arithmetic mean)".

Average problems come in two categories: Single and Multiple
a) Single average problems are generally easier and can be solved using the formula
$Avg = \dfrac{sum-of-terms}{\#-of-terms}$, although the pie still works! To assist on some problems, you can just use converting equations. For example, if the problem states that they want you to find the average price **per** gallon from a list, just take the price **divided by** the number of gallons.
b) Multiple average problems are usually more difficult and involve the use of the average pie to organize your data.

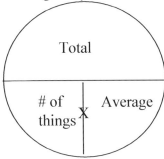

***Don't worry about plugging in here
Average pie's will do the job for you!***

If the average (arithmetic mean) of a, 2a, and b is 2a, what is b in terms of a?

(A) a
(B) $\dfrac{3}{2}a$
(C) 2a
(D) 3a

The average (arithmetic mean) age of a certain group of 20 people is 12 years. If 4 additional people are included in the group, then the average age of the 24 people is 14 years. What is the average age of the 4 additional people?

(A) 14
(B) 16
(C) 20
(D) 24

If a is the average (arithmetic mean) of x and 5, b is the average of 2x and 7, and c is the average of 2x and 18, then what would be the average in terms of x if x and 18 were taken away from the other terms?

(A) x-7
(B) x+3
(C) x
(D) x+10

Modes: the members of a set that occur the most frequently.

Medians: The middle term of a set of **arranged from least to greatest**. In an odd set, there is one median. In an even set, the median is the average of the two middle terms. For example:

In a set of 7 integers: 4, 8, 9, 15, 16, 16, 19
The Mode is 16, and the Median is 15

In a set of 6 integers: 4, 8, 9, 16, 16, 19
The Mode is 16 and the Median is the AVERAGE of the two middle terms.
Median = $\frac{9+16}{2} = \frac{25}{2} = 12.5$

Whenever you see a median question, PUT THE NUMBERS IN ORDER! If the list is too large, find out how many terms there are and the middle term number will contain the median.

15, 44, 0, a, 55, 20, 30

In the list above, the value of a is the same as the value of one of the other numbers listed. What are all the possible values for the median of these seven numbers?

(A) 20 only
(B) 25 only
(C) 30 only
(D) 20 and 30 only

The following examples refer to the chart below:

Grades	East High School	West High School
A's	123	100
B's	97	141
C's	100	160
D's	88	70
F's	71	50

What is the median grade for all the students surveyed?

(A) A
(B) B
(C) C
(D) D

If all A's were entered at 90's, all B's as 80's, all C's as 70's, etc… How would the range be affected if all the D's and F's weren't counted?

(A) The range would decrease by 10
(B) The range would become $\frac{1}{4}th$ of the median
(C) The range would be $\frac{1}{4}th$ of the mode
(D) The range would be $\frac{3}{4}th$ of the average

Mean, Median, Mode, and Range	
Test #1	
Sec. 3	
Sec. 4	12 , 14
Test #2	
Sec. 3	
Sec. 4	19
Test #3	
Sec. 3	
Sec. 4	32, 35
Test #4	
Sec. 3	
Sec. 4	29

Read Data and Make Conclusions:

This final section of Arithmetic should serve as a cumulative review of many topics that have led up to this point, namely the following:

1. Ratios:
    a. Remember that $a \text{ to } b = a/b$
    b. You will be using conversion factors on some of these as well.
    c. You will also be using proportions to convert. Start with the scale factor (initial ratio) and then compare it to the actual value; remember the cross product rule!
2. Bite Sized Pieces:
    a. Attack the problems in chunks.
    b. Remember to circle/underline any important information that will help you solve the problem.
    c. Some information is useless, look only for what you need!
    d. If the problem is needed you to add up the information (HINT HINT), then do it!
3. Means and Medians:

Read Data and Make Conclusions	
Test #1	
Sec. 3	
Sec. 4	7, 23, 27
Test #2	
Sec. 3	
Sec. 4	11, 18, 20
Test #3	
Sec. 3	
Sec. 4	15
Test #4	
Sec. 3	
Sec. 4	10, 11, 21

Algebra 1

Solving Equations/Inequalities

Coming into this section, it is expected that you are able to solve simple algebraic equations. It is also expected that you know how to work the following simple fraction rules:

$$\frac{a}{b} + \frac{c}{d} = \frac{ad+bc}{bd} \qquad \frac{a}{b} \times \frac{c}{d} = \frac{ac}{bd}$$

Therefore, I would like to bring up a few specific solving techniques that will be applied on the SAT.

Solve the following:

ex) $\frac{5}{3}x + 3 = 18$

ex) $w + 4 = 5w$, find $3w$.

ex) $2x + 7 \leq 4x + 11$

ex) $|2x - 5| = 9$

ex) $\left|\frac{4}{5}x + 7\right| > 9$

ex) $\frac{x+2}{x-2} = 6$

Literal Equations: Some problems will ask you to solve for a specific variable. While the question will tell you what variable to solve for, sometimes the wording can be confusing; don't worry though, because you just need to look at the answer choices and you can see which variable you will be solving for.

ex) $V = \frac{4\pi r^3}{3}$; solve for r

ex) $T = \frac{2l}{5x}$; solve for x

ex) $y = 2x^2 + bx + 3$; solve for x

ex) $\frac{a-b}{b} = c$; solve for b

Solving Equations/Inequalities	
Test #1	
Sec. 3	7
Sec. 4	8, 9, 11
Test #2	
Sec. 3	1, 12, 16
Sec. 4	3, 21, 22
Test #3	
Sec. 3	2, 17
Sec. 4	7, 13
Test #4	
Sec. 3	1, 10
Sec. 4	19

Slope

When it comes to slope, you need to know the following:
$$\text{Slope} = \frac{rise}{run}$$ which can also be written as $$Slope = \frac{y_2 - y_1}{x_2 - x_1}$$

Slope also has another name - rate of change.

Remember that a slope is a fraction, and that this fraction can be written as a rate (hence rate of change).

If line *l* passes through $(-2, b)$ and $(5, -3)$, and if line *l* is parallel to line *m*, which has a slope of $-\frac{9}{4}$, what is the value of *b*?

(A) $-\frac{3}{2}$
(B) $\frac{51}{4}$
(C) $-\frac{9}{4}$
(D) $\frac{2}{3}$

Jose was measuring the height of the water in his cup while adding ice cubes. When Jose originally added 4 ice cubes, the height of water in his cup was 6 inches. When Jose added two more ice cubes, the height rose to 6.35 inches. What was the initial height of the water in the cup in inches?

(A) 5
(B) 5.1
(C) 5.2
(D) 5.3

The following chart gives the height of a child over a given time period:

Year	2008	2010	2011	2015
Height	48 in	55in	58in	69in

Which of the following statements correctly compares the average rates at which the height changes over time?

(A) The average rate of change is greatest between 2011 and 2015
(B) The average rate stays the same throughout each interval
(C) The average rate is 3 inches per year in between 2008 and 2011
(D) The average rate is the greatest between 2008 and 2010

Slope	
Test #1	
Sec. 3	
Sec. 4	22
Test #2	
Sec. 3	6
Sec. 4	25, 27
Test #3	
Sec. 3	
Sec. 4	26
Test #4	
Sec. 3	7, 20
Sec. 4	

Equations of Lines

For this section, you will need to know the following linear equations:

1. Slope-intercept form: $y = mx + b$
   a. m = the SLOPE of the line
      i. The SAT labels these with the words **each and per**
   b. b = the Y-INTERCEPT (0,b)
      i. The SAT labels these with the words **initial and amount PER week/month/etc..**
      ii. The SAT likes to use slope-intercept equations in the form $y = b - mx$, where you have an initial amount, and you lose a set amount over each time period.
2. Standard Form: $Ax + By = C$
   a. This form is useful when finding equations of lines when given x and y intercepts.
   b. Made up of two rates
      i. If a word problem includes two rates (remember, look for words such as **each and per**), you are going to be setting up a standard form equation.
3. Translations of Lines: $y = m(x - h) + k$
   a. Translated from $y = x$
      i. Slope = 1
      ii. The y-intercept passes through the origin (0,0)
   b. m = slope
   c. − h: move the parent graph right h
   d. + h: move the parent graph left h
   e. − k: move the parent graph down k
   f. + k: move the parent graph up k
4. Parallel and Perpendicular Lines
   a. Parallel lines have the SAME slope
   b. Perpendicular lines have OPPOSITE RECIPRICAL slopes
5. Direct and Indirect Variation
   a. Direct variation equation: $y = kx$
   b. Indirect variation equation: $y = \frac{k}{x}$
6. Linear inequalities
   a. Typically you will be working only with slope-intercept form and standard form inequalities
   b. Words that mean "greater than" or "greater than or equal to"
      i. At least (≥), at or above (≥), above (>), etc…
   c. Words that mean "less than" or "less than or equal to"
      i. At most (≤), at or below (≤), below (<), etc…

If x is directly proportional to y and x = 6 when y = 12, what is the value of y when x = 3?

(A) $\frac{1}{6}$
(B) $\frac{1}{2}$
(C) 2
(D) 6
(E) 24

If x is inversely proportional to y and x = 6 when y = 12, what is the value of y when x = 3?

(A) $\frac{1}{6}$
(B) $\frac{1}{2}$
(C) 2
(D) 6
(E) 24

In the xy-plane, line *l* passes through the point (0, -1) and is parallel to the line with equation -4x + 3y = 12. If the equation of line *l* is y = ax + b, what is the value of a + b ?

In the xy-plane, line *l* passes through the point (0, -1) and is perpendicular to the line with equation -4x + 3y = 12. If the equation of line *l* is y = ax + b, what is the value of a + b ?

John is buying vanilla and peach yogurt cups and has $45 to spend. Vanilla yogurt cups cost $5 each and peach yogurt cups cost $2 each. Let *x* stand for vanilla and *y* stand for peach yogurt cups. Which inequality shows how many cups John can buy?

(A) $x + y < 45$
(B) $5x + 2y \leq 45$
(C) $5x + 2y \leq 7$
(D) $5x + 2y < 45$

John is buying vanilla and peach yogurt cups with his friend Lucas. John bought 2 vanilla yogurt cups for *x* dollars each. Lucas bought 1 peach yogurt cup, which was $1.00 more than the price of one vanilla yogurt cup. If John and Lucas split the cost of the yogurt evenly and each paid 7% sales tax, which of the following represents the amount of dollars that each of them paid?

(A) $1.14x + .535$
(B) $.14 + .07x$
(C) $3.21x + 1.07$
(D) $.535 + 1.605x$

The monthly membership fee at Shape Up Gym is $10.50. The cost of attending a yoga class at the gym is $1.25 each. For one month, Claire's bill was $18. How many yoga classes did Claire attend?

(A) 2
(B) 4
(C) 6
(D) 8

Which of the following equations represent the line that passes through (2,1) and (5,-3)?

(A) $y = -\frac{2}{3}(x - 2) + 1$
(B) $y = -\frac{4}{3}(x + 2) + 1$
(C) $y = -\frac{2}{3}(x + 2) - 1$
(D) $y = -\frac{4}{3}(x - 2) + 1$

What is the equation of the line that passes through (7,0) and (0,-4)?

(A) $7x - 4y = 3$
(B) $7x - 4y = 28$
(C) $4x - 7y = 28$
(D) $4x - 7y = -3$

Jill has a phone plan that includes a certain amount of gigabytes of data per month. The amount of data that she has left per month can be estimated with the equation $D = 6 - .2t$, where D is the amount of data that she has remaining and t is the number of days in the month. What is the meaning of the 6 and .2 in the equation?

(A) Jill will use up her data is 6 days at .2 gigabytes per day
(B) Jill initially had 6 gigabytes and uses .2 gigabytes per day
(C) Jill loses .2 gigabytes from her 6 gigabyte plan per month
(D) Jill loses data at 6 gigabytes per day and will run out of data in only .2 days

Equations of Lines	
Test #1	
Sec. 3	3, 4, 6, 12
Sec. 4	2, 15, 16
Test #2	
Sec. 3	3
Sec. 4	1, 4, 8, 12, 28, 35
Test #3	
Sec. 3	8
Sec. 4	4, 8, 14, 24
Test #4	
Sec. 3	8, 12
Sec. 4	1, 2, 17, 27

Systems of Equations/Inequalities

When solving a system of equations, remember the three methods used for solving:

1. Graphing
    a. When you graph a system of equations, the **intersection point** represents your solution. If the lines are **parallel**, there is **no solution**, and if the lines are the **same**, then there are **infinite solutions**.
    b. When solving systems of inequalities, most problems will require a graph. You can graph each function, then use a test point to determine where to shade.
2. Substitution
    a. This method is preferred when one equation is solved for a variable, can easily be solved for a variable, or both equations are already solved for the same variable.
3. Elimination
    a. This method is preferred when both equations are in standard form. You want to get of the coefficients to a variable to match; in order to do that, you may need to multiply one or both equations.

When working through this section, remember the rules for finding the equations of lines and converting equations, as they will be needed again!

Finally, half of these questions are located in the NO CALCULATOR section, and some require some extensive arithmetic. As we work through these examples, do NOT use your calculator, and as you work through to problems, remember to take note of what section you are on, because practicing these problems with a calculator when you are not supposed to have one will NOT help you properly prepare for test day.

$$3x + 2y = 14$$
$$x - 2y = 2$$

What is the solution (x,y) to the system of equations above?

(A) (5,2)
(B) (2,-7)
(C) (4,1)
(D) (-5,1)

$$2x + y = 1$$
$$3x + 4y = 14$$

What is the solution (x,y) to the system of equations above?

(A) (-2,5)
(B) (7,-2)
(C) (-1,4)
(D) (5,-1)

$$8x + 4y = 12$$
$$4x - 3y = 11$$

According to the system of equations above, what is the value of x?

The graph of a line has a slope of 3 and contains the point (3,4). The graph of a second line passes through the points (4,-7) and (-2,-1). If the two lines intersect at the point (h,k), what is the value of $\frac{h}{k}$?

(A) $\frac{1}{2}$
(B) $-\frac{1}{3}$
(C) $-\frac{1}{7}$
(D) -3

$$4x + y \leq 2$$
$$y \leq 2x$$

According to the system of inequalities above, what is the maximum value of y?

$$3x + 2y > -2$$
$$x + 2y \leq 2$$

According to the system of inequalities above, which quadrant contains the solutions to the system?

(A) Quadrants I, II, and III
(B) Quadrants II and IV
(C) Quadrants I, II, and IV
(D) All Quadrants

If the question is asking you to find values that would give you either **infinitely many solutions** or **no solutions**, start by putting both equations in slope intercept form. There are shortcuts as well, which I will show you!

$$ax - by = 12$$
$$4x - 3y = 72$$

In the system of equations, above, a and b are constants. If the system has infinitely many solutions, what is the value of $\frac{b}{a}$?

$$ax - 4y = 12$$
$$4x - 3y = 15$$

In the system of equations, above, a is a constant. If the system has no solution, what is the value of a?

(A) $4/3$
(B) $16/3$
(C) $-4/3$
(D) $-16/3$

Many word problems use the following setup for their equations:
- Equation 1: A "quantity" → $x + y = C$
- Equation 2: A relationship ($x = C \pm y$) or a "cost" type of equation ($Ax + By = C$)

Not every word problem follows this model, but it is a popular one that you need to be aware of.

Larry, Curly, and Moe have a total of $79. Larry has $5 more than Curly, and Moe has twice as much money as Larry has. How much money does Curly have?

A gas station sells two types of gasoline: regular at $2.20 per gallon and premium at $3.00 per gallon. At the end of the business day the cashier finds that receipts totaled $680 and that 280 gallons of gas was sold. How many gallons of regular gas was sold?

Systems of Equations/Inequalities	
Test #1	
Sec. 3	9, 11, 18
Sec. 4	18, 19, 28
Test #2	
Sec. 3	2, 9, 20
Sec. 4	9, 34
Test #3	
Sec. 3	6, 9, 19
Sec. 4	18, 29, 30, 31, 36
Test #4	
Sec. 3	3, 11, 13, 19
Sec. 4	6, 30

Finding a Graph to Match a Situation

This next problem set is a simple application of the skills that you have learned throughout this unit. When reading charts and matching graphs to information, pay attention to when a graph is increasing and decreasing, as well as the rate at which it is doing so. In addition, if a problem is describing a situation, and they don't provide the picture, DRAW IT.

Finding a Graph to Match a Situation	
Test #1	
Sec. 3	
Sec. 4	1
Test #2	
Sec. 3	
Sec. 4	
Test #3	
Sec. 3	
Sec. 4	1, 3
Test #4	
Sec. 3	
Sec. 4	8

GEOMETRY

Only a small percentage of the math problems on the SAT involve Geometry. Luckily, you will not need to do any proofs, and most of the formulas you need are given to you at the beginning of every math section!

Geometry Basics/Volume

While there are many different concepts to know in Geometry, which we will go over one by one, here are some concepts that translate throughout this section:
1. Know the rules! Don't ever get a question wrong just because you don't know a basic Geometry rule!
2. If there is a figure, show all the information.
3. If there is no figure, draw your own.
4. Decide what formulas are needed to solve the problem and WRITE THEM DOWN
5. If you do all this and get really stuck, you can BALLPARK
    a. Figure must be drawn to scale
    b. Round off numbers like pi and square roots.

Here are the formulas that are given to you at the beginning of every math test. Don't forget about these!

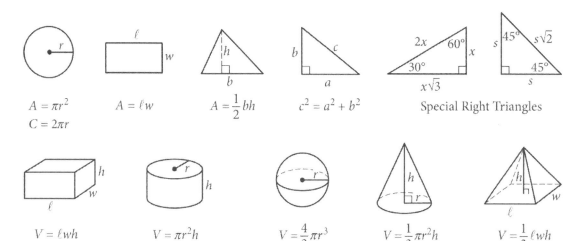

The number of degrees of arc in a circle is 360.
The number of radians of arc in a circle is 2π.
The sum of the measures in degrees of the angles of a triangle is 180.

The volume of a right circular cylinder is 125π cubic inches. If the height and base radius of the cylinder are equal, what is the height of the cylinder?

(A) 5 inches
(B) 10 inches
(C) 15 inches
(D) 25 inches

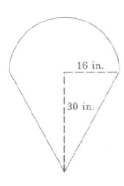

A cross-section of a massive ice cream cone is shown above and is made up of a right circular cone with the ice cream filling the cone completely and forming a hemisphere on top of the cone. Which of the following is the closest to the volume of ice cream in terms of ft^3?

(A) 23.1
(B) 17.3
(C) 9.3
(D) 1.1

In addition, here are some concepts that you may find helpful:

1)

- AB = CD means AB has the SAME LENGTH as CD.
- The Midpoint of a segment means the middle.
- Bisect means "Cut in Half".
- Angle Bisector means "two equal angles"

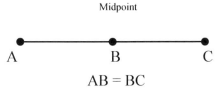

Points A, B, C, D, and E lie on a line, in that order, so that C is the midpoint of $\overline{AD}$ and D is the midpoint of $\overline{CE}$. If AB = 2 and AE = 18, what is the length of $\overline{BD}$?

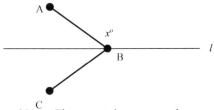

Note: Figure not drawn to scale

In the figure above, line l bisects ∠ABC, and the measure of ∠ABC is 20°. What is the value of x?

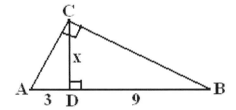 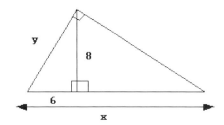

Triangles	
Test #1	
Sec. 3	17
Sec. 4	
Test #2	
Sec. 3	18
Sec. 4	
Test #3	
Sec. 3	18
Sec. 4	
Test #4	
Sec. 3	16
Sec. 4	

Circles

The SAT loves testing copious amounts of different concepts in relation to circles. Don't worry though, we will review them all here.

1) Angles

- A Circle Contains $360°$ OR 2π radians
- To convert from degree to radians, just use the following proportion:

$$\frac{degree\ angle}{360°} = \frac{radian\ angle}{2\pi}$$

Convert the following:

$120°$ to radians $\frac{\pi}{3}$ radians to degrees $\frac{2\pi}{7}$ radians to degrees

It doesn't hurt if you know the unit circle, although it's not required.

2) Arcs

- The SAT will ask you to find either the length or area of an arc. When working on arc problems, just plug in the following formulas (where r is the radius and x is the central angles of the circle).

$$Area_{sector} = \frac{x}{360}\pi r^2 \text{ or } \frac{x}{2\pi}\pi r^2$$

$$Length_{sector} = \frac{x}{360}2\pi r \text{ or } \frac{x}{2\pi}2\pi r$$

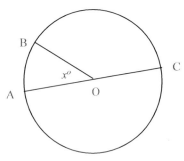

Note: Figure not drawn to scale

The figure above shows a circle with center O and diameter $\overline{AC}$. if OB = 4 and the area of arc BC is 2π, then x =

(A) 30
(B) 45
(C) 120
(D) 135

In a circle with center O, central angle BOC has a measure of $\frac{7\pi}{6}$ radians. The length of the sector formed by central angle BOC is what fraction of the circumference of the circle?

3) Additional topics

- A diameter of a circle forms a $180°$ angle.
- A tangent line is a line that touches a circle at exactly one point. Any radius drawn from that tangent point forms a $90°$ angle.

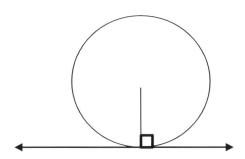

4) The equation of a circle

- The equation of a circle centered at (0,0) with radius r
  - $x^2 + y^2 = r^2$
- The equation of a circle centered at (h,k) with radius r
  - $(x - h)^2 + (y - k)^2 = r^2$

In order to solve some problems that require the use the equation of a circle, you will need to know how to **complete the square**. Completing the square is required because the equation of a circle contains perfect squares. If the equation that you are given does not contain perfect squares, you will need to make them yourself. Lets practice.

$$x^2 + y^2 + 2x + 6y = 15$$

The equation of a circle is shown above. What is the center of the circle?

(A) (1,3)
(B) (1,9)
(C) (-1,-3)
(D) (-1,-9)

$$x^2 + y^2 - 4x - 12y - 9 = 0$$

The equation of a circle is shown above. What is the radius of the circle?

(A) 6
(B) 7
(C) 36
(D) 49

Which of the following is the equation of a circle with center (3,5) and a radius with the endpoint (0,2)?

(A) $(x + 3)^2 + (y + 5)^2 = 9$
(B) $(x - 3)^2 + (y - 5)^2 = 9$
(C) $(x + 3)^2 + (y + 5)^2 = 18$
(D) $(x - 3)^2 + (y - 5)^2 = 18$

Circles	
Test #1	
Sec. 3	
Sec. 4	24
Test #2	
Sec. 3	19
Sec. 4	24, 36
Test #3	
Sec. 3	
Sec. 4	34
Test #4	
Sec. 3	
Sec. 4	24, 36

Algebra 2/Advanced Topics

Functions and Applications with Functions

To begin with, you must know and understand that $f(x) = y$; this is stated "f OF x equals y", not "f times x equals y". For example:

Let the function f be defined by $f(x) = 2x - 7$ for all values of x. If $f(3) = t$, what is the value of $f(t)$?

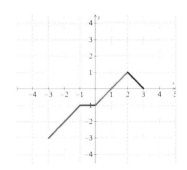

The complete graph of function f is shown in the graph above. For what value of x is the value of $f(x)$ at its maximum?

(A) -3
(B) 1
(C) 2
(D) 3

You must also understand Composition of Functions. Composite functions are those in the form $f(g(x))$, although sometimes they can be written in the form $(f \circ g)(x)$ (not typically shown on the SAT, but know this form just in case). You may be forced to evaluate the composite functions or you may have to "undo" to "decompose" the composites. Lets try it.

If $f(x) = 3x - 5$ and $g(x) = 2 - x^2$, what is the value of $f(g(-4))$?

(A) 49
(B) 13
(C) -11
(D) -47

If $h(x) = \sqrt{x} + 1$ and $g(x) = \sqrt{x}$, what would be an appropriate value for $f(x)$ if $h(x) = f(g(x))$?

(A) $f(x) = x$
(B) $f(x) = \sqrt{x} + 1$
(C) $f(x) = x + 1$
(D) $f(x) = x^2 + 1$

And now for the meat of this section. When you are given a function that represents a real life model, DON'T SKIP TO THE END OF THE PROBLEM. You must CAREFULLY read through the information (as boring as it may be). While you are reading, start by paying attention (and possibly even making notes) of what each variable represents. In addition, you must pay attention to the UNITS being used, as they may change in the question itself. Finally, make sure you look for any values that are ALREADY being given to you; if you miss that very important piece of information, you will find yourself stuck when trying to solve the problem. If the function contains a variable that represents a constant, then you may be allowed to plug in your own constant!

While these types of problems can and will show up anywhere, they usually show up in pairs and at the end of section 4. That is the format that we will stick with for our practice problems.

The following two examples refer to the following information

$$v(t) = \frac{1087\sqrt{273 + t}}{K}$$

$$f(t) = \frac{5}{9}t + 32$$

The speed of sound in feet per second through any given temperature of air is given by the function v, where t is the temperature in degrees Celsius and K is a constant equal to 16.52. Temperature f in degrees Fahrenheit can be found using the formula $f(t)$, where t is still degrees Celsius.

What would be the speed of sound v if the temperature was 35°F?

By what percent does the speed of sound change when the temperature changes from 32°F to 37°C?

Functions and Applications with Functions	
Test #1	
Sec. 3	10
Sec. 4	17
Test #2	
Sec. 3	
Sec. 4	10, 26, 33, 37, 38
Test #3	
Sec. 3	1
Sec. 4	10, 11, 16, 37, 38
Test #4	
Sec. 3	2, 4
Sec. 4	5, 14, 16, 32, 35

Quadratic Functions

When working with quadratic functions, you need to be aware of multiple forms and formulas. Here are the two ways that a quadratic function can be written:

Standard Form
$y = ax^2 + bx + c$

a, b, and c are constants

If $a > 0$, parabola opens up and the vertex is the minimum

If $a < 0$, parabola opens down and The vertex is the maximum

c = The y-intercept

Vertex: $(\frac{-b}{2a}, f\left(\frac{-b}{2a}\right))$

Vertex Form
$y = a(x - h)^2 + k$

If $a > 0$, parabola opens up and the vertex is the minimum

If $a < 0$, parabola opens down and the vertex is the maximum

Vertex: (h, k)

In order to go from **standard form** to **vertex form**, you will need to be able to complete the square (we first reviewed this in the circle section in Geometry).

Solutions to Quadratics: Regardless of what you call it, a solution to a quadratic represents the y-intercept, or zero of the function (the x-value when **y = 0**).
1. Zeroes
2. x-intercepts
3. Roots
4. Factors
    a. A factor may be written in the form $x - 2$ as opposed to $x = 2$.

FOIL/Distributive Property: Some of the easier questions will just ask you to multiply out the quadratic. Use the FOIL and Distributive Property rules to simplify it!

Factoring: Know the following special factors.
- $x^2 - y^2 = (x + y)(x - y)$
- $(x + y)^2 = x^2 + 2xy + y^2$
- $(x - y)^2 = x^2 - 2xy + y^2$
- Also, don't forget to pull out GCF's when applicable.

Quadratic Formula: You MUST know this by heart. This is going to be tested on every SAT!

$$x = \frac{-b \pm \sqrt{b^2 - 4ac}}{2a}$$

$$h(t) = -16t^2 + 42t$$

The function above represents the approximate height, h, in feet, of an object t seconds after it is launched upward from the ground with an initial velocity of 42 ft/sec. After approximately how many seconds will the object hit the ground?

(A) 1.7
(B) 2.1
(C) 2.6
(D) 3.1

$$y = x^2 - 6x + 7$$

Which is the following is equivalent to the quadratic function listed above?

(A) $y = (x-7)(x+1)$
(B) $y = (x-7)(x-1)$
(C) $y = (x+3)^2 - 2$
(D) $y = (x-3)^2 - 2$

$$y = 2x^2 - 7x - 15$$

Which of the following lists a function that contains the same roots as those in the parabola above?

(A) $(2x+3)(x+5)$
(B) $(2x+3)(x-5)$
(C) $(2x-3)(x+5)$
(D) $(2x-3)(x-5)$

Which of the following equations has a graph whose vertex is a maximum and y is always less than or equal to 4?

(A) $y = (x-1)^2 + 4$
(B) $y = (x+3)^2 - 4$
(C) $y = -(x+3)^2 + 5$
(D) $y = -(x-5)^2 + 3$

$$y = x^2 - 6x + 1$$

Which of the following are roots to the quadratic function listed above?

(A) $3 \pm 2\sqrt{2}$
(B) $6 \pm 2\sqrt{2}$
(C) $-3 \pm 4\sqrt{2}$
(D) $-6 \pm \sqrt{32}$

$$y = a(x+1)(2x-3)$$

If a is a non-zero constant in the equation above and the vertex of the parabola is located at (b,c), which of the following is equivalent to c?

(A) $-\frac{5}{4}a$
(B) $-\frac{2}{15}a$
(C) $0a$
(D) $-\frac{25}{8}a$

In the xy-plane, the parabola with the equation $y = (x-6)^2 + 7$ intersects with the linear equation $y = 56$. What is the smallest possible solution of $x + 10$?

If a and b are positive integers and $a^2 - b^2 = 7$, what is the value of a?

Quadratic Functions	
Test #1	
Sec. 3	15, 16
Sec. 4	25 , 30
Test #2	
Sec. 3	10, 13, 17
Sec. 4	7, 29
Test #3	
Sec. 3	7, 10, 12, 14
Sec. 4	
Test #4	
Sec. 3	5 , 15
Sec. 4	28

Polynomials

The Polynomial section will be eerily similar to the previous section on Quadratics. Here are some of the concepts that translate over and a couple of new ideas:

Solutions to Polynomials: Regardless of what you call it, a solution to a polynomial represents the y-intercept, or zero of the function (the x-value when **y = 0**).
1. Zeroes
2. x-intercepts
3. Roots
4. Factors
    a. A factor may be written in the form $x - 2$ as opposed to $x = 2$.

FOIL/Distributive Property: Some of the easier questions will just ask you to multiply out the polynomial. Use the FOIL and Distributive Property rules to simplify it!

Combining Polynomials:
- **Adding:** Adding Polynomials is easy enough. Look for like terms and combine them using the appropriate operation.
- **Subtracting:** This is where the issues arise. When subtracting polynomials, be sure to distribute the negative throughout the second polynomial.
- **Dividing:** Dividing polynomials can be done through Polynomial Long Division; this is a fairly difficult concept to explain in words, so you will see it in the examples below. It does help, however, to know the Reminder Theorem.

Remainder Theorem: *If $f(x)$ is divided by $x - c$ with remainder r, then $f(c) = r$*

Factoring: Know the following special factors (even more important in this section).
- $x^2 - y^2 = (x + y)(x - y)$
- $(x + y)^2 = x^2 + 2xy + y^2$
- $(x - y)^2 = x^2 - 2xy + y^2$
- Factor by Grouping when given <u>4 terms</u> (example below)
- Also, don't forget to pull out GCF's when applicable.

If the graph of function *f*, in the *xy*-plane, has zeroes at $\pm\frac{1}{2}$, which of the following could define *f*?

(A) $f(x) = (x - 4)(x + 4)\left(x^2 + \frac{1}{4}\right)$
(B) $f(x) = 4x^4 + 2x^2 + 1$
(C) $f(x) = 16x^4 - 8x^2 + 1$
(D) $f(x) = 16x^4 - 4$

$$x^3 - 4x^2 - 18x + 72$$

What is the sum of the solutions to the equation above?

$(2x^2 - 4x + 5) - (x - 4)^2$

If the expression above is rewritten in the form $ax^2 + bx + c$, where a, b, and c are constants, what would be the value of $b + c$?

(A) -15
(B) 7
(C) 9
(D) 17

How many <u>distinct</u> zeroes are there in the graph of following function listed above?

(A) 1
(B) 2
(C) 3
(D) 4

$12a^4 + 36a^2b^2 + 27b^4$

Which of the following is equivalent to the expression listed above?

(A) $(2a^2 + 3b^2)^2$
(B) $3(2a + 3b)^2$
(C) $3(4a^2 + 9b^2)^2$
(D) $3(2a^2 + 3b^2)^2$

Which of the following is the remainder when $2x^2 - x - 3$ is divided by $x - 3$?

(A) 14
(B) 12
(C) 10
(D) 13

$f(x) = 3x^5 + 5x^4 - 4x^3 + 7x + 3$

If the remainder when function f is divided by $x + 2$ is 5, what is $f(-2)$?

No Calculator

Polynomials	
Test #1	
Sec. 3	5
Sec. 4	29
Test #2	
Sec. 3	4
Sec. 4	
Test #3	
Sec. 3	13, 16
Sec. 4	6, 12, 33
Test #4	
Sec. 3	18
Sec. 4	12, 25

Exponential Functions

Exponential functions come from the concept of geometric sequences, where the operation required to get from one term to the next is to multiply or divide the output. For examples:

Linear FunctionExponential Function
(Arithmetic Sequence of Numbers)(Geometric Sequence of Numbers)

x	y
1	2
2	5
3	8
4	11

x	y
1	2
2	6
3	18
4	54

Exponential _____

x	y
1	2
2	-1
3	-4
4	-7

x	y
1	2
2	$2/3$
3	$2/9$
4	$2/27$

Exponential _____

Parent Graph: $f(x) = ab^x$

a = "initial" or "starting" point (y-intercept)
b = rate of change
  If $b > 1$, exponential growth
  If $0 < b < 1$, exponential decay

Many SAT questions that relate to exponential functions are concept problems. Look for terms such as "increasing/decreasing by x% per year" or phrases such as "decay" ,or obviously, the word "exponential" in the question or answer choices.

Important Note: Many exponential questions will give you rates in terms of percentages. When using percentages, you must convert them into decimal form to use in the exponential equation. The SAT will typically use decaying models to trick you. For example, if an object decays by 17% per year, your rate will be $1 - .17 = .83$.

Exponents Rules: When not dealing with exponential functions, you will be asked to apply the exponent rules. Remember these!

Exponent Rules: $a^m \bullet a^n = a^{m+n}$ $\dfrac{a^m}{a^n} = a^{m-n}$ $(a^m)^n = a^{mn}$

$a^{-m} = \dfrac{1}{a^m}$ $\dfrac{1}{a^{-m}} = a^m$ $a^{\frac{m}{n}} = \sqrt[n]{a^m}$

ex) $2^3 \times 2^5 =$

ex) $(2^3)^4 =$

ex) $\dfrac{a^3}{a^5} =$

ex) $\dfrac{16^x}{2^y} =$

ex) $\sqrt[3]{y^2} =$

ex) $\left(\dfrac{x^6 y^2}{x^7 y}\right)^{-2} =$

A radioactive isotope decays at an annual rate of 23%. If the initial amount of the isotope is 250 grams, which of the following models the remaining amount, in grams, after t years?

(A) $f(t) = .23(250)^t$
(B) $f(t) = .77(250)^t$
(C) $f(t) = 250(.23)^t$
(D) $f(t) = 250(.77)^t$

x	y
0	3
1	9
3	81
6	2187

Which of the following equations best models the data above?

(A) $y = 3(9)^x$
(B) $f(t) = 9(3)^x$
(C) $f(t) = 3(3)^x$
(D) $f(t) = 9(9)^x$

Exponential Functions	
Test #1	
Sec. 3	14
Sec. 4	
Test #2	
Sec. 3	14
Sec. 4	
Test #3	
Sec. 3	3
Sec. 4	21, 28
Test #4	
Sec. 3	
Sec. 4	13, 15, 20, 37, 38

Radical/Rational Functions

Rational Functions are functions with negative exponents or *x*'s in the denominator. In short, they are functions in fraction form, so in order to work with these functions, you need to remember the following concepts:

$$\frac{a}{b} + \frac{c}{d} = \frac{ad+bc}{bd} \qquad \frac{a}{b} \times \frac{c}{d} = \frac{ac}{bd} \qquad \frac{\frac{a}{b}}{\frac{c}{d}} = \frac{a}{b} \times \frac{d}{c}$$

We reviewed these concepts earlier, but now they will be used in function form. Lets try some.

Ex) Simplify the following

a) $\frac{x^2+2x-3}{x^2+8x+16} \cdot \frac{3x+12}{x-1}$

b) $\frac{x-4}{x^2-4} \div \frac{x^2-3x-4}{x^2+5x+6}$

c) $\frac{1}{x^2-1} - \frac{2}{(x+1)^2}$

d) $\frac{\frac{x}{y} - \frac{y}{x}}{\frac{1}{x^2} - \frac{1}{y^2}}$

e) $\frac{2}{\sqrt{2}}$

f) $\frac{1}{1+\sqrt{2}}$

Radical Functions are functions that contain roots, or fractional exponents. On the SAT, you are most likely going to see square root functions. When solving, follow this simple process:

1) Isolate the radical
2) Square both sides (or raise both sides to the same power as the root)
3) Solve for the variable
    a. Linear equations: isolate the variable
    b. Quadratic equations: set = 0 and factor
4) Check for extraneous solutions
    a. For example, examine the following equation
    $$\sqrt{x} = 2$$

Lets try some:

Ex) Solve the equations

a) $2x - 1 = -\sqrt{2 - x}$

b) If $b = 3\sqrt{2}$ and $4b = \sqrt{32x}$, solve for x.

Radical/Rational Functions	
Test #1	
Sec. 3	13, 20
Sec. 4	
Test #2	
Sec. 3	5, 15
Sec. 4	
Test #3	
Sec. 3	
Sec. 4	
Test #4	
Sec. 3	9
Sec. 4	

Complex Numbers

Complex numbers are numbers with real and imaginary components; they are written in the following format:

$$a \pm bi, \text{ where } i = \sqrt{-1}$$

When solving complex number problems, you will need to use the rational and radical concepts from the prior section. However, you also need to be aware of the different iterations of i. Since these problems don't show up too much in this problem set, lets try a couple before you start your practice set:

$i = \sqrt{-1}$ $\qquad i^2 =$ $\qquad i^3 =$ $\qquad i^4 =$ $\qquad i^5 =$

$i^{47} =$ $\qquad\qquad i^{84} =$ $\qquad\qquad i^{26} =$

Simplify the following:

a) $\frac{6}{3i}$ $\qquad$ b) $\frac{1}{2+i}$ $\qquad$ c) $\frac{3+2i}{4+3i}$

Complex Numbers	
Test #1	
Sec. 3	2
Sec. 4	
Test #2	
Sec. 3	11
Sec. 4	
Test #3	
Sec. 3	
Sec. 4	
Test #4	
Sec. 3	
Sec. 4	

Line/Curve of Best Fit

At this point, we have just about learned all that we need to attack the SAT. In this final section you will be fitting lines and curves to data. There are just a couple of concepts to be aware of before attacking this final section.

Correlation:
- Strong correlation: The data points closely match the curve of best fit
- Weak correlation: The data points don't closely match the curve of best fit
- Negative correlation: The data trends downward from left to right
- Positive correlation: The data trends upwards from left to right

ex) Give examples of the following:

a) Strong Positive Correlation

b) Weak Negative Correlation

c) No correlation

Line/Curve of Best Fit	
Test #1	
Sec. 3	
Sec. 4	5
Test #2	
Sec. 3	
Sec. 4	14
Test #3	
Sec. 3	
Sec. 4	20
Test #4	
Sec. 3	
Sec. 4	

NOTES:

NOTES:

Homework:

Date: Assignment:

Homework:

Date: Assignment:

Made in the USA
Lexington, KY
15 June 2016